6 May – 4 June 1994

AVIGDOR ARIKHA

Works 1992 – 93

Most works are for sale: Prices upon request

Marlborough Fine Art (London) Ltd
6 Albemarle Street, London W1X 4BY
Telephone: 071⁄629 5161
Telefax: 071⁄629 6338

00006495

PAINTINGS

1

Anne in Red and Black, 24 January 1993
oil on canvas
100 × 81 cm, $38\frac{3}{8} \times 31\frac{7}{8}$ in.
signed l.l. and dated on reverse

3

Etching Tools and Plates, 25 December 1992
oil on canvas
46 × 33 cm, $18\frac{1}{8} \times 13$ in.
signed u.r. and dated on reverse

4

Tea Time, 21 November 1992
oil on canvas
38 × 46 cm, $15 \times 18\frac{1}{8}$ in.
signed l.r. and dated on reverse

5

Stool and Shoes, 31 January 1993
oil on canvas
73 × 60 cm, $28\frac{3}{4} \times 25\frac{5}{8}$ in.
signed l.l. and dated on reverse

6

Leon Wieseltier, 16 October 1992
oil on canvas
81 × 100 cm, $31\frac{7}{8} \times 39\frac{3}{8}$ in.
signed u.r. and dated on reverse

7

Evening Attributes, 6 February 1993
oil on canvas
46.1 × 55 cm, $18\frac{1}{8} \times 21\frac{5}{8}$ in.
signed u.l. and dated on reverse

9

Richard Morphet, 28 February 1992
oil on canvas
46 × 55 cm, $18\frac{1}{8} \times 21\frac{5}{8}$ in.
signed l.l. and dated on reverse

10

Four Jars, 23 December 1992
oil on canvas
38 × 61 cm, 15×24 in.
signed l.r. and dated on reverse

12

Four Kinds of Hats, 10 January 1993
oil on canvas
65 × 81 cm, $25\frac{1}{2} \times 31\frac{7}{8}$ in.
signed l.r. and dated on reverse

13

Seven Tomatoes, 15 November 1992
oil on canvas
38 × 46 cm, $15 \times 18\frac{1}{8}$ in.
signed l.l.

15

Ipsius, 12 January 1993
oil on canvas
55 × 46 cm, $21\frac{5}{8} \times 18\frac{1}{8}$ in.
signed l.r. and dated on reverse

16

View on Ratisbonne, 12 August 1993
oil on canvas
49 × 36 cm, $19\frac{1}{4} \times 14\frac{1}{8}$ in.
signed l.c. and dated on reverse

17

Moira Shearer and Ludovic Kennedy, 28 February 1993
oil on canvas
81 × 100 cm, $31\frac{7}{8} \times 39\frac{3}{8}$ in.
signed u.r. and dated on reverse
Edinburgh, Scottish National Portrait Gallery
(not exhibited)

19

Parka and Umbrella, 3 February 1993
oil on canvas
81 × 100 cm, $31\frac{7}{8} \times 39\frac{3}{8}$ in.
signed l.l. and dated on reverse

20

Daydream, 19 February 1993
oil on canvas
97 × 130 cm, $38\frac{1}{8} \times 51\frac{1}{8}$ in.
signed u.r. and dated on reverse

21

A Frugal Meal, 13 February 1993
oil on canvas
81 × 65 cm, $31\frac{7}{8} \times 25\frac{1}{2}$ in.
signed l.l. and dated on reverse

23

Gan Rehavia, 4 August 1993
oil on canvas
64 × 50 cm, $25\frac{1}{8} \times 19\frac{5}{8}$ in.
signed l.l. and dated on reverse.

25

Near the Window, 13 November 1992
oil on canvas
130 × 97 cm, $51\frac{1}{8} \times 38\frac{1}{8}$ in.
signed l.r. and dated on reverse

8
Five Brushes, 9 January 1993
pastel on wove paper
22 × 50 cm, $8\frac{5}{8}$ × $19\frac{5}{8}$ in.
signed l.r. dated l.l.

11
Self-Portrait in Jeans, 29 August 1992
pastel on hand-made Japan paper
80 × 29 cm, $31\frac{1}{2}$ × $11\frac{3}{8}$ in.
signed l.l. dated u.r.

14
Books, December 1993
pastel on emery paper
31.6 × 44.7 cm, $12\frac{1}{2}$ × $17\frac{1}{2}$ in
signed l.r.

22
Self-Portrait Seated, at Work, 24 December 1992
pastel on tinted brown board
65 × 50 cm, $25\frac{5}{8}$ × $19\frac{5}{8}$ in.
signed l.l. dated u.l.

2
Anne in Winter, Seated, 23 February 1992
soft graphite on hand-made Japan paper
71.8 × 63 cm, $26\frac{1}{4}$ × $24\frac{7}{8}$ in.
signed u.r. dated u.l.

18
Two Poets (C.K. Williams and Adam Zagajewski), 4 June 1993
charcoal on Kawasaki paper
65 × 88.5 cm, $25\frac{1}{2}$ × $34\frac{7}{8}$ in.
signed l.l. dated u.l.

24
The Twins (Ruth and Tamar), 11 August 1993
soft graphite on BFK Rives
76 × 56 cm, $29\frac{7}{8}$ × 22 in.
signed l.c. dated u.c.

26
Nude Woman with a Finger at her Mouth, 31 August 1992
soft graphite on hand-made Japan paper
97 × 63 cm, $38\frac{1}{8}$ × $24\frac{7}{8}$ in.
signed l.r. dated u.l.

27
Sleeping Nude, 3 February 1992
soft graphite on hand-made Japan paper
63 × 67.8 cm, $24\frac{7}{8}$ × $26\frac{5}{8}$ in.
signed l.c. dated u.c.

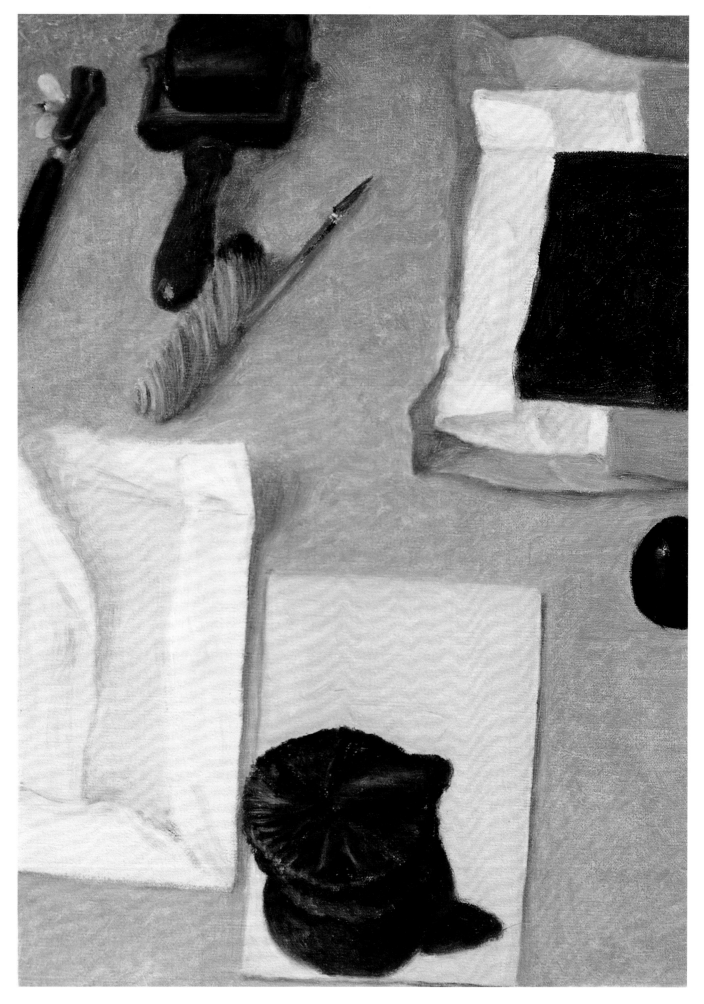

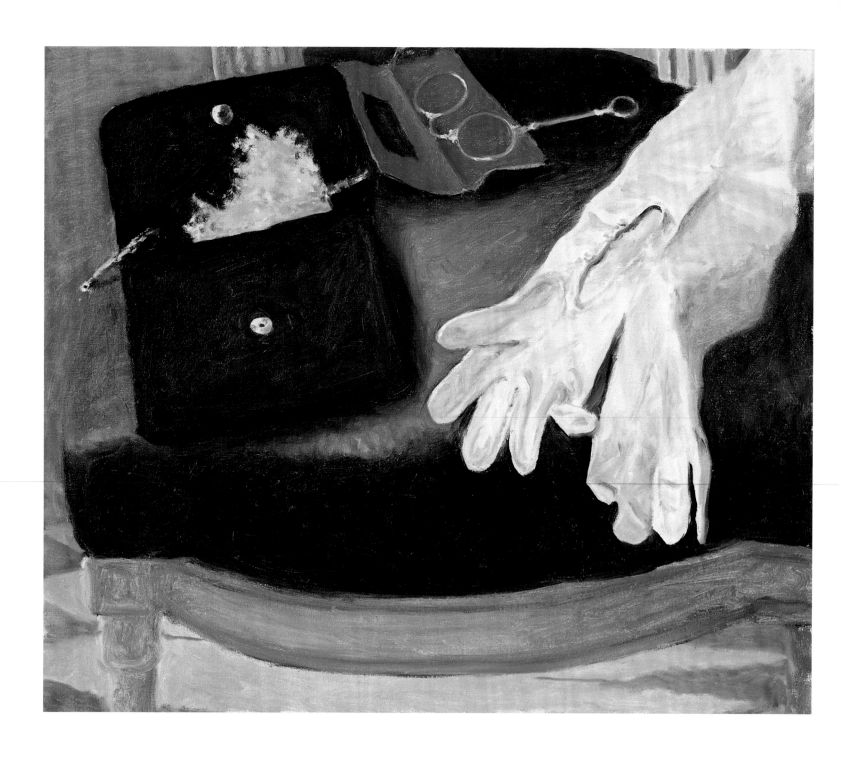

24

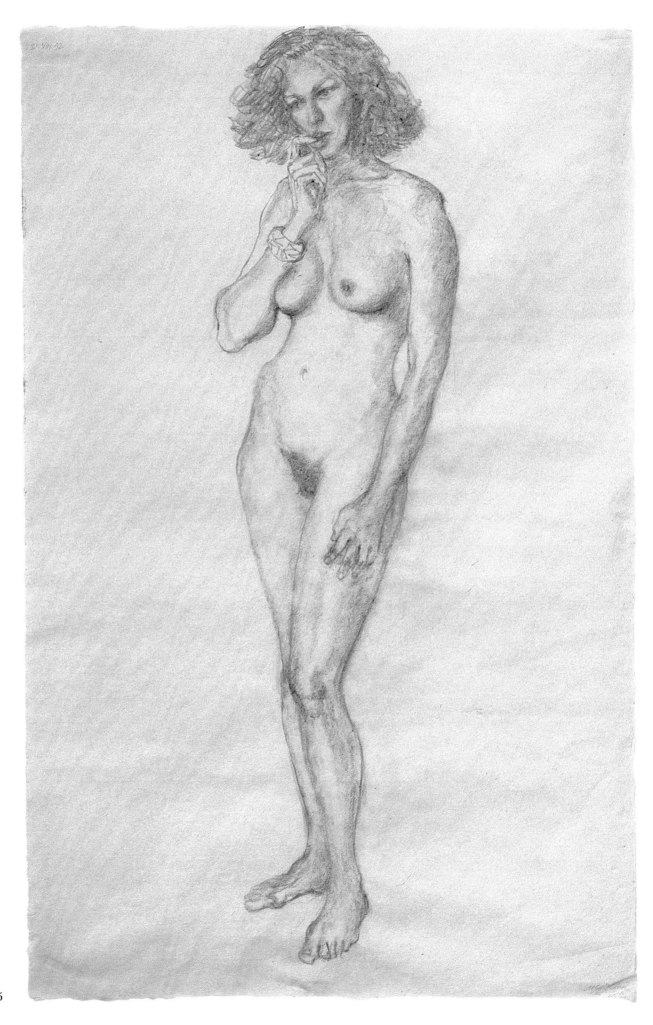

26

EXHIBITIONS, WRITINGS, OTHER ACTIVITIES AND SELECTED BIBLIOGRAPHY
FOR THE PERIOD 1952–1993

1952	Tel Aviv, *Galeria Zeira*, Paintings and Drawings
1953	Jerusalem, *Artists' House*, Paintings, Drawings and Illustrations
	Jerusalem, *The Bezalel National Museum*, Paintings, Drawings and Woodcuts
1954	Stockholm, *Galerie Moderne*, Paintings and Drawings
	Copenhagen, *Athenæum Kunsthandel*, Drawings and Book-illustrations
1955	Paris, *Galerie Furstenberg*, Paintings and Drawings
1956	London, *Matthiesen Gallery*, Paintings and Drawings
1957	Paris, *Galerie Furstenberg*, Paintings
1959	London, *Matthiesen Gallery*, Paintings, Gouaches and Drawings
1960	Amsterdam, *Stedelijk Museum*, Paintings, Gouaches and Watercolours
1961	Paris, *Galerie Karl Flinker*, Paintings, Gouaches and Drawings
1966	Jerusalem, *Israel Museum*, Paintings 1963–6 and Drawings 1947–66
1967	Paris, *Galerie Claude Bernard*, Drawings 1965–6
1970	Paris, *Centre National d'Art Contemporain*, Drawings 1965–70
1972	Tel Aviv, *Gordon Gallery*, Paintings and Drawings
	Los Angeles, *Los Angeles County Museum of Art*, Drawings 1965–72
	New York, *Marlborough Gallery*, Drawings 1965–72
1973	Syracuse, NY, *Everson Museum*, Drawings 1965–72
	Fort Worth, Texas, *Fort Worth Art Center Museum*, Drawings 1965–72
	Tel Aviv, *The Tel Aviv Museum of Art*, Paintings 1957–65 and 68 (abstract period)
1974	Houston, Texas, *Janie C Lee Gallery*, Drawings and Prints
	London, *Marlborough Fine Art*, Drawings and Prints
1974–9	Paris, *CNAC-MNAM-Centre Pompidou*, circulating exhibit of Prints:
	1974: Boulogne-sur-Mer, *Musée des Beaux-Arts et d'Archéologie*; Saint-Quentin-en-Yvelines, *Chapelle de la Villedieu*; 1975: Le Mans, *Musée Tessé*; Nice, *Ecole Internationale d'Art Décoratif*; Dôle, MJC; 1976: Mitry-Mory, *Municipalité*; Brive-la-Gaillarde, *Foyer Culturel*; Saint-Cloud, *MJC;* Annecy, *MJC*; Mandelieu-la-Napoule, *MJC*; Verberie, *MJC*; Bordeaux, *Renaissance du Vieux Bordeaux*; 1977: Mougins, *Maison pour Tous*; Saumur, *Bibliothèque Municipale*; Tourcoing, *Ecole des Beaux-Arts*; Vieux Condé, *Lycée Technique*; Gennevilliers, *Société Creusot-Loire*; Gérardmer, *MJC*; Chamonix, *Bibliothèque Municipale*; Bastia, *Musée d'Ethnographie Corse*; 1978: Grasse, *Fédération Régionale des MJC*; Sorgues, *Comité d'Animation de la Bibliothèque*; Compiègne, *Lycée Pierre d'Ailly*; Castres, *Musée Goya*; Lyon, *Espace Lyonnais d'Art Contemporain*; Myridan, *Amicale Laïque*; Evry, *Bibliothèque de l'Agora*; 1979: Köln (Cologne), *Institut Français*; Aachen, *Institut Français*; Essen, *Institut Français*; Grenoble, *Bibliothèque Municipale*
1975	Paris, *Cabinet des Estampes, Bibliothèque Nationale*, Prints
	New York, *Marlborough Gallery*, Paintings and Watercolours
1976	London, *Victoria & Albert Museum*, 'Samuel Beckett – Drawings, Prints and Illustrations'
1977	Zürich, *Marlborough Gallery*, Paintings, Watercolours and Drawings
	Zürich, *Galerie Amstutz*, Prints
1978	London, *Marlborough Fine Art*, Paintings, Watercolours and Drawings
1979	Houston, Texas, *Janie C Lee Gallery*, Paintings, Watercolours and Drawings
	Washington, *The Corcoran Gallery*, Paintings
	Paris, *FIAC Marlborough Stand*, Paintings and Watercolours
1980	Paris, *Galerie Berggruen*, Prints and Drawings
	New York, *Marlborough Gallery*, Paintings, Watercolours and Drawings
1981	Dijon, *Musée des Beaux-Arts*, Paintings, Watercolours and Drawings
1982	London, *Marlborough Fine Art*, Paintings and Drawings
1983	New York, *Marlborough Gallery*, Paintings, Pastels and Drawings
1984	New York, *Marlborough Gallery*, Drawings
1985	New York, *Marlborough Gallery*, Paintings
1986	Tel Aviv, *Tel Aviv University Gallery*, Prints
	London, *Marlborough Fine Art*, Paintings, Pastels and Drawings
1987	Venice, California, *LA Louver Gallery*, Paintings and Drawings
1988	Tokyo, *Marlborough Fine Art*, Paintings, Pastels and Drawings
	New York, *Marlborough Gallery*, Paintings, Pastels and Drawings
1990	London, *Marlborough Fine Art*, Paintings, Pastels and Drawings
1992	New York, *Marlborough Gallery*, Paintings, Pastels and Drawings

1954 Milan, 10th *Triennale* (awarded Gold Medal for the Rilke illustrations)
1959 Paris, 1st *Biennale*
1962 Venice, *Biennale* (Israeli pavilion)
1964–6 New York, *MOMA*, 'Art Israel', circulating exhibition in the USA and Canada
1967 Saõ Paulo, *Biennale* (Israeli pavilion)
1975–6 Los Angeles, *Los Angeles County Museum of Art*, 'European Painting in the 70s'
Saint-Louis, *Art Museum*; Madison, Wis., *Elvehjem Art Center*
1976 Paris, *Festival d'Automne*, 'Nouvelle Subjectivité'
1977 Paris, *CNAC-MNAM-Centre Pompidou*, Cabinet graphique, Acquisitions 1971–6
London, *National Portrait Gallery*, new acquisitions
1978 Paris, *Cabinet des Estampes, Bibliothèque Nationale*, 'L'Estampe Aujourd'hui'
Paris, *Grand Palais*, 'L'Art Moderne dans les Musées de Province'
1979 Paris, *CNAC-MNAM-Centre Pompidou*, 'Oeuvres Contemporaines des Collections
Nationales'
1980 Paris, *Musée des Arts Décoratifs*, 'La famille des portraits'
1981 New York, *Jewish Museum*, 'Artists of Israel 1920–1980'
1982 Los Angeles, *Los Angeles County Museum of Art*, 'The M & D Blankfort Collection'
Paris, *Fondation des Arts Graphiques*, 'La lithographie en France des origines à nos
jours'
Venice, *Biennale, International Pavilion*, 'Arte come arte...'
Vienna, *Museum des XX^{ten} Jahrhunderts*, 'Paris 1960–1980'
1983 Paris, *Grand Palais*, 'Raphaël et l'Art Français'
1984 Washington, *The Hirshhorn Museum*, 'Drawings 1974–1984'
Houston, Texas, *Janie C Lee Gallery*, 'Master Drawings 1928–1984'
London, *Marlborough Graphics*, 'A Circle: Portraits and Self-portraits by Arikha,
Auerbach, Kitaj, Freud'
Tokyo, *Marlborough Fine Art*, 'Masters of Contemporary Figuration'
New York, *Janie C Lee Gallery*, 'Master Drawings 1879–1984'
1985 Washington, *The Hirshhorn Museum*, 'Representation Abroad'
Frankfurt, Kassel, *Kunstverein*; Wien, *Museum Moderner Kunst*, 'Vom Zeichnen'
1987 Jerusalem, *Israel Museum*; Marseille, *Musée Cantini*, 'Peindre dans la lumière de la
Méditerranée'
New York, *Janie C Lee Gallery*, 'Ink drawings'
1988 New York, *Janie C Lee Gallery*, 'Master Drawings 1877–1987'
1991 New York, *Janie C Lee Gallery & Kate Ganz*, 'Master Drawings 1520–1990'
Paris, *FIAC Marlborough Stand*, 'Arikha, Auerbach, Bacon, Kitaj'
1993 Paris, *Musée du Louvre*, 'Copier Créer'
Madrid, *Galeria Marlborough*, 'Arikha, Auerbach, Kitaj'

SELECTED BOOK-GRAPHICS (ORIGINAL LIMITED EDITIONS)
6 Litografier till Dvärgen av Pär Lagerkvist, Stockholm, Sandbergs Bokhandel, 1954, 50 copies
Samuel Beckett, *L'issue*, six colour aquatints, Paris, Georges Visat, 1968, 154 copies
Samuel Beckett, *The North*, three etchings, London, Enitharmon Press, 1972, 137 copies
Samuel Beckett, *Au loin un oiseau*, five aquatints, New York, Double Elephant Press, 1973, 126
copies
Anne Atik, *Words in Hock*, one aquatint, London, Enitharmon Press, 1974, 30 copies
Facing Mount Zion, seven lithographs, Tel Aviv, Gordon Gallery, 1978, 113 copies
Anne Atik, *Offshore*, 1 lithograph (and 1 by R B Kitaj), London, Enitharmon, 1991, 85 copies

SELECTED ILLUSTRATED BOOKS
Rainer Maria Rilke, *Cornet*, Hebrew translation by Ytzhak Shenhar (*Massa ahavato umitato shel
hakornet Christoph Rilke*), 35 pen drawings (1951–52), Tarshish Books, Jerusalem 1953
Awarded the *Gold Medal* of the Xth Triennial, Milan, 1954
Ernest Hemingway, *The Old Man and the Sea*, Hebrew, 6 pen drawings (1953), Am Oved, Tel
Aviv, 1953
Hayim Nahman Bialik, *Safiah*, Hebrew, 15 lithographs and pen drawings, the Bialik Institute,
Jerusalem, 1955
Nicolas Gogol, *The Dead Souls*, translated by Arthur Adamov, French, 13 felt drawings, La
Guilde du Livre, Lausanne, 1956
Binyamin Tammuz, *Holot Hazahav*, Hebrew, 9 pen drawings (1957), Sifriat Poalim, Tel Aviv,
1958
Samuel Beckett, *Nouvelles et textes pour rien*, 6 pen drawings (1957), Les Editions de Minuit, Paris,
1958
S J Agnon, *Kelev Houtzot*, Hebrew, 5 wood-cuts (1953), 6 pen drawings (1955) and 5 brush
drawings (1958), Tarshish Books, Jerusalem, 1961
T Carmi, *Nahash Hanehoshet*, 6 inks (1960), Tarshish Books, Jerusalem, 1961

ARCHITECTURAL WORKS
Woonsocket, R I, USA, Bnei Israel Synagogue, 30 stained-glass windows (1961)
Jerusalem, Municipality, City Council Hall, 6 stained-glass windows (1968, installed in 1972)
Jerusalem, Beith Hahayal, 1 mosaic (1970)

STAGE DESIGN
Endgame by Samuel Beckett, directed by Alvin Epstein, The Samuel Beckett Theater, Theater
Row, New York, 1984

PROJECT
'Project for an Environmental Structure (Labyrinth) to be erected in a Park or Public Garden',
1971 in *A Report on the Art and Technology Program of the Los Angeles County Museum of Art*,
Los Angeles, 1971

BOOKS BY ARIKHA

Peinture et regard, Écrits sur l'art 1965–1990, Hermann, Éditeurs des Sciences et des Arts, Collection Savoir sur l'art, Paris, 1991, 256 pp

Nicolas Poussin: The Rape of the Sabines, The Museum of Fine Arts, Houston and the Art Museum, Princeton University, published by the MFA, Houston, 1982, 68 pp

idem: modified version in *Nicolas Poussin lettres et propos sur l'art, textes réunis et présentés par Anthony Blunt, avant-propos de Jacques Thuillier suivi de réflexion sur Poussin par Arikha*, Collection Savoir, Hermann, Paris, 1989

J A D Ingres: Fifty Life Drawings from the Ingres Museum of Montauban, The Museum of Fine Arts, Houston and the Frick Collection, New York, published by the MFA, Houston, 1986, 120 pp

ESSAYS, ARTICLES AND STATEMENTS BY ARIKHA (IN CHRONOLOGICAL ORDER)
(titles marked with an * are reprinted [sometimes modified] in *Peinture et regard*)

'Bein melakha leomanuth', *Massa*, Tel Aviv, Dec 1952, no 22 p 2 (Hebrew)

'Kain Noak Abraham, israels nya literatur' *BLM*, Stockholm, vol 23 no 4, April 1954, pp 289–93 (written in German, Swedish translation by Johannes Edfelt)

'Kryat Hareik', *Qeshett*, Tel Aviv, 1959, vol 5, pp 80–95 (Hebrew)

Untitled statement, in *Le jardin des arts*, Paris, November 1961, vol 84, p 60

'Halal o halal ruah', *Kav*, Jerusalem, 1965, vol 2, pp 22–3 (Hebrew)

*'Peinture et regard', *Les lettres nouvelles*, Paris, May–June 1966, pp 75–7

'Peinture: Le neuf ou l'unique?', *Les lettres nouvelles*, Paris, March–April 1968, pp 144–6

Untitled statement, in *Arts primitifs dans les ateliers d'artistes*, Musée de l'Homme, Paris, 1967

'Al rishumei Ingres', *Kav*, Jerusalem, 1968, vol 8, pp 72–3 (Hebrew)

'Samuel Beckett', *Haaretz*, Tel Aviv, 7 Nov 1969 (Hebrew)

* *Two Books: The Apocalypse of Saint-Sever and Matisse's Jazz*, Los Angeles County Museum of Art, 1972 (exh. brochure)

idem: 'Beatus & Jazz', French version in *Connaissance des arts*, no 468, Paris, Feb 1991, 16 c pl, pp 26–41

idem: 'Beatus & Jazz de Matisse y el Apocalipsis de San Severo', Spanish translation (by Leticia Leduc) in *Saber Ver*, Año 1, no 3, Mexico, March 1992, 13 c pl, pp 6–22

Statement, in *European Painting in the 70s: New Work by 16 Artists*, Los Angeles County Museum of Art, 1975 (exh. cat.)

Statement, in *Avigdor Arikha: Paintings and Watercolors*, Marlborough Gallery, New York, 1975 (exh. cat.); reprinted in German in *Avigdor Arikha: Ölbilder-Aquarelle-Zeichnungen*, Marlborough Galerie, Zürich, 1977 (exh. cat.); reprinted in *Arikha: Oeuvre gravé*, Institut Français, Cologne, Jan–Feb 1979 (exh. announcement)

*'De la saccade au damier' (on Cézanne), *Art International*, vol 21, no 3, May–June 1977

'A propos du terme Palestine' (published under the pseudonym A Vigo), *Pouvoirs*, Paris, 1978, vol 7, pp 157–62

'Un livre de Samuel Beckett et Avigdor Arikha: Au loin un oiseau. Note d'Avigdor Arikha', *La revue de l'art*, Paris, 1979, no 44, p 103

Untitled text, in *Facing Mount Zion*, seven lithographs, The Gordon Galleries, Tel Aviv, 1978 (Hebrew and English)

*'L'Enlèvement des Sabines de Poussin', Musée du Louvre, RMN, Paris, 1979 (*Petit journal* accompanying the exhibition *Dossier no 17 du Département des Peintures du Musée du Louvre, 10 mars – 21 mai 1979* curated by this author)

* *Ingres: 53 dessins sur le vif du Musée Ingres et du Musée du Louvre*, Israel Museum, Jerusalem, 1981, 180 pp (French and Hebrew)

Ingres – Dessins sur le vif: 52 dessins du Musée Ingres de Montauban, Musée des Beaux-Arts, Dijon, 1981, 80 pp

Untitled statement, in *L'écriture et la peinture*, CNAC Magazine, Centre Georges Pompidou, Paris, Nov–Dec 1982, pp 12–13

*'De l'abstraction en peinture', *Cahiers du Musée National d'Art Moderne*, Centre Georges Pompidou, Paris, 1982, vol 10, pp 208–11

*Untitled statement on Pierre Bonnard, *Petit journal Bonnard*, Musée National d'Art Moderne, Centre Georges Pompidou, Paris, 1984 (exh. brochure)

Untitled statement, in '*Culture et démocratie aujourd'hui*', a colloquy in the French Senate, *France-Forum*, Paris, April–June 1985, vol 219–20, p 26

Untitled statement: in *Vom Zeichnen Aspekte der Zeichnung 1960–1985*, exh. cat., Frankfurter Kunstverein, Frankfurt-am-Main, 1986, p 20

*'Pintor Real' (book review on J Brown's *Velázquez, Painter and Courtier*), *The New York Review of Books*, vol XXXIII, no 17, New York, Nov 6, 1986, pp 27–35

idem: 'Pintor Real', *Diario 16 (Culturas)* Madrid, 30 Nov 1986, pp II–V (Spanish translation)

Untitled, in *Art Libraries Journal*, vol II no 3, Preston, Great Britain, 1986, p 14

*'A propos de la lumière', *Le débat*, vol 44, Paris, March–May 1987, pp 164–6

idem: 'On Light', *Antique*, London, summer 1987, p 47

idem: enlarged version in *Art in America*, Jan 1988, pp 102–4 (editorial errors)

idem: ''bizkhut haor hativ'iy', *Kav*, Jerusalem, Jan 1989, pp 88–9 (Hebrew)

*'An Offshore Glance at Painting in Britain', *Art International*, no 1, Paris, autumn 1987, pp 62–4

'The End of the History of Art?', letter, *The Times Literary Supplement*, no 4, 411, London, October 16–22, 1987, p 1139

*On Peter Paul Rubens (editorial title: 'Painter with Portfolio'), book review on C White's *Peter Paul Rubens*, *The New Republic*, Washington, March 28, 1988, pp 33–7

*'Jacques-Louis David: Les licteurs rapportent à Brutus les corps de ses fils', *Rendez-vous en France*, Dossier, no 3, Paris, Dec 1988, pp 5–8

idem: in *Connaissance des arts*, Paris, Nov 1989, no 453, pp 72–81

idem: 'David's Brutus', English version, with an introductory note in *The Journal of Art*, vol 2 no 1, Turin, Sept–Oct 1989, pp 8–9 (footnotes deleted)

'An open letter to art historians', *The Journal of Art*, vol 1, no 3, Turin, Feb–March 1989, p 19 (editorial modifications)

*'Giacometti's Code', *The New York Review of Books*, vol XXXVI, no 8, New York, May 18, 1989, pp 20–24

'Remarques à propos de la politique artistique', *Commentaire*, vol 49, pp 107–9, Paris, March 1990

'Un point pour le grand souffle' (on Samuel Beckett), in *Samuel Beckett, Revue d'esthétique*, hors série 1990, pp 3–5

idem: Hebrew version (translated by Helith Yeshurun) in HADARIM, vol 9, Tel-Aviv, summer 1990, pp 71–2

*'From Prayer to Painting', published under the title of 'On Transgressing the Prohibition of Images', *The Journal of Art*, vol 3, no 3, New York, Dec 1990, p 32

'The Mysteries of Spanish Golden Age Drawing', a talk with Barbara Rose in *The Journal of Art*, vol 4, no 7, New York, Sept 1991

'Painting and the end of communism' – 'Brushes with death' (editorial title and subtitle), *The New Republic*, Washington, Dec 16, 1991, pp 40–2

idem: Hebrew translation 'Igul hu tamid igul' in *Maariv (hashavua)*, Tel-Aviv, 17 Jan 1992, pp 54–5

idem: French version 'De l'utopie avant-gardiste', in *Connaissance des arts*, Paris, April 1993

'Quelle Modernité?', *Commentaire*, no 63, Paris, autumn 1993, pp 617–22

SELECTED INTERVIEWS

BARZEL, Amnon: 'Sihot im Avigdor Arikha', *Haaretz*, Tel Aviv, 18 Feb 1972 (Hebrew)

BARZEL, Amnon: 'Hakmihah Letzayer min Hateva', *Haaretz*, Tel Aviv, 5 Sept 1975 (Hebrew)

BOWLES, Patrick: 'Avigdor Arikha – An Interview and Portfolio presented by Patrick Bowles' *The Paris Review*, vol 33, winter–spring 1964–5, pp 22–9

JODIDIO, Philip: 'Trois opinions sur la situation culturelle en France: 1. Avigdor Arikha', *Connaissance des arts*, no 427, Paris, Sept 1987, pp 58–61

MAURIES, Patrick: 'Sur le vif', *L'âne le magazine Freudien*, no 26, Paris, April–June 1986, pp 14–15

ROSE, Barbara: Avigdor Arikha interviewed by Barbara Rose, in *Avigdor Arikha Oil Paintings, Watercolours, Drawings* (exh. cat.), Marlborough Fine Art, London, May–June 1978; reprinted in *Avigdor Arikha Drawings, Watercolors and Paintings*, Janie C Lee Gallery, Houston, Texas, Feb–March 1979

SAHUT, Marie-Catherine: 'L'enlèvement des Sabines de Poussin', interview, *La revue du Louvre*, Paris, 1979, no 2, p 142

SELDIS, Henry J: 'A Conversation with Avigdor Arikha', *Arts Magazine*, New York, 1975, vol 50, no 2, pp 53–6

SHANNON, Joseph: 'An Interview with Avigdor Arikha', *Arts*, New York, Jan 1984, pp 130–33

TUCHMAN, Maurice: 'A Talk with Avigdor Arikha', *Art International*, May–June 1977, vol 21, no 3, pp 12–16

VIATTE, Germain: *Avigdor Arikha – Germain Viatte: extrait d'un entretien (20 juillet 1973)*, travelling exhibition brochure Arikha 39 Gravures, Centre National d'Art Contemporain, Paris, 1973

RADIO

A talk on the Collection of the São Paulo Museum, BBC Hebrew Service, London, July 1954, (7 min)

An interview with Daniel Le Comte, Radio France, France Culture, Paris, 22 Oct 1976 (27 min)

An interview with Connie Goldman, National Public Radio, Washington DC, 19 July 1979 (12 min)

An interview with Amnon Ahineomi, Kol Israel, Jerusalem, 6 July 1980 (one hour)

Nicolas Poussin – a joint talk with Pierre Rosenberg; interviewer: Pierre Descargues, Radio France, France Culture, 11 Feb 1982 (26 min)

On Antoine Watteau – interview with Pierre Descargues, France Culture, 12 Nov 1984 (12 min)

An interview produced by Sam Collyns and Adrian Velicu, BBC Radio 3 'New Premises' (series V), London, 7 Dec 1986 (13 min) (inaccuracies in presentation)

Zeitzeichen – on Henri Cartier-Bresson, West Deutscher Rundfunk 2, 22 Aug 1988 (German, 7 min within 15)

An interview with Richard Thomson, 'Third Ear', produced by Judith Bumpus, BBC Radio 3, 7 April 1989 (26 min)

On Sumerian art – Participation in *'Emission spéciale Grand Louvre'*, France Culture, Paris, 1 April 1989

TELEVISION AND FILM

An interview with Terry Wehn-Damish, 'Zigzag' ANTENNE2 Paris, 28 Oct 1976 (10 min)

On Chardin (shared with Pierre Rosenberg), 'Zigzag' ANTENNE2, Paris, (?) Feb 1979 (7 min within 26 min)

On Poussin's 'L'Enlèvement des Sabines', Télévision Belge, (?) April 1979

Le portrait, 'Zigzag', ANTENNE2, Paris, 30 Jan 1980 (7 min within 26 min)

On Monsieur Bertin by Ingres, Télévision Française TF1, within the televised news broadcast, Paris, (?) Aug 1980 (3 min)

A brief interview about the portrait of HM Queen Elizabeth, the Queen Mother, Breakfast News, BBC1, ITV, and STV, London and Edinburgh, 4 Aug 1983

'Du vif au vrai', a film directed by Daniel Le Comte, Télévision Française TF1, Paris, 12 April 1985 (26 min)

On Henri Cartier-Bresson, Indian National Television, New Delhi, 1985, (date?)

A short talk within the televised news, *televisia limudit*, Tel-Aviv (date?) Jan 1986 (7 min, Hebrew)

Five short films: *Velázquez' Meninas* (9½ min); *Poussin's Deluge* (8 min); *David's Brutus* (11 min); *Caravaggio's Saint Andrew* (12 min); *Vermeer's Woman Holding a Balance* (13 min); directed and produced by Sarah Stein (sponsored by *Minda de Gunzburg, The ASDA Foundation*), New York, 1985 (distributed by the *American Federation of Arts*, New York)

An interview with Robert Hughes in *Saturday Review*, directed by Rosemary Bowen-Jones, BBC2, 8 March 1986

Das Hungrige Auge AVIGDOR ARIKHA, a film by Erwin Leiser (60 min), German television networks, first broadcast: 2 Sept 1991 (SWF, SF), *Saarländischer Rundfunk* (German and English versions)

ARIKHA ON VELAZQUEZ, a film directed by Patricia Wheatley, produced by Keith Alexander, BBC2 (40 min), London, 24 May 1992

AVIGDOR ARIKHA, a film ('*Omnibus*') directed by Patricia Wheatley, BBC1 (50 min), first broadcast: London, 27 October 1992; first broadcast on Israel Television 18 Oct 1992

LECTURES

Peindre aujourd'hui, a lecture, Ecole Nationale Supérieure des Beaux-Arts, Paris, 16 Dec 1981

Poussin's Deluge, a seminar, Department of Art History, Université de Genève, 4 June 1982

Nicolas Poussin and the Classical Ideal, Museum of Fine Arts, Houston, 24 Jan 1983

Some late works of Nicolas Poussin, Princeton University, The Art Museum (McCormick Hall), 1 May 1983

A propos de Deux Pastels de Degas (Portraits d'Amis sur Scène, 1879, Baigneuse allongée sur le Sol, 1886–8), Musée d'Orsay (part of the series "Voir et Apprendre à Voir"), Paris, 30 October 1988

An informal seminar and a public lecture on *'Disruptures in styles'*, The Graduate School of Fine Arts, University of Pennsylvania, Philadelphia, 14 and 15 Feb 1989

Disruptures in style – painting today, School of Art, Yale University, New Haven, 20 Feb 1989

Prix des arts, des lettres et des sciences – Fondation du Judaïsme français, the laureat's lecture, Paris, 25 May 1989

On David's 'Brutus' and his 'unfinished' portraits, *Bretey Memorial Lecture, University of Manchester*, 17 May 1990

BOOKS/MONOGRAPHS

ARIKHA Texts by Richard Channin, André Fermigier, Robert Hughes, Jane Livingston, Barbara Rose and Samuel Beckett. Interviews by Barbara Rose, Joseph Shannon and Maurice Tuchman. 224 pp, 106 col pl, 83 b & w, Hermann, Paris / Thames & Hudson, London, 1985

Arikha, by Duncan Thomson, 256 pp., 214 colour and b & w plates, London, Phaidon Press, 1994

LIMITED ORIGINAL EDITION

Avigdor Arikha: Boyhood Drawings made in Deportation – Seven facsimile reproductions of drawings made at age thirteen in Nazi concentration camps (1942–3) with an introduction, 18 pp box, English edition of 200, French edition of 100 signed and numbered copies; printed in collotype by *Daniel Jacomet*, Paris, 1971, published by Alix de Rothschild for the benefit of Youth Aliyah

EXHIBITION CATALOGUES (IN CHRONOLOGICAL ORDER)

ARTISTS' HOUSE JERUSALEM, 3–24 Jan 1953, *Paintings, Drawings and Illustrations*, foreword by Binyamin Tammuz, Hebrew and English, brochure 8 pp

NATIONAL MUSEUM BEZALEL, Jerusalem, 5–22 Sept 1953, *Peintures, dessins et bois*, foreword by Mordechai Narkiss, Hebrew and French, folder

GALERIE MODERNE, Stockholm, 24 April–7 May 1954, checklist, Swedish, folder

ATHENAEUM KUNSTHANDEL, Copenhagen, 1–15 Sept 1955, *Tegninger, grafik og bogkunst*, introduction Peter P. Rohde, Danish, folder, 1 repr.

MATTHIESEN GALLERY, London, 5–28 April (first London exhibition), 1956, folder

GALERIE FURSTENBERG, Paris, 2–16 April 1957, *Peintures récentes*, text by Jean Wahl, folder

MATTHIESEN GALLERY, London, 8 April–2 May 1959, *Paintings, gouaches and drawings*, with a poem (French) by Samuel Beckett, brochure, 8 pp, 1 col. repr., cover

STEDELIJK MUSEUM, Amsterdam, Oct–Nov 1960, cat. no 248 (joint with Panter), Dutch, brochure 12 pp, 7 b&w, 1 col. repr.

GALERIE KARL FLINKER, Paris, 11 Oct–4 Nov 1961, untitled brochure, 1 col. (cover), 2 b&w repr.

ISRAEL MUSEUM, Jerusalem, *Paintings 1963–66, Drawings 1947–1966*, Sept–Oct 1966, introduction by Yona Fischer, Hebrew and English, brochure, 12 pp, 4 b&w repr.

GALERIE CLAUDE BERNARD, Paris, Jan–Feb 1967, *Arikha – dessins*, announcement, with the text 'Pour Avigdor Arikha' by Samuel Beckett

CENTRE NATIONAL D'ART CONTEMPORAIN, Paris, *Dessins 1965–1970*, 8 Dec 1970–18 Jan 1971, foreword by Samuel Beckett, introduction by Barbara Rose, two texts by the artist, 64 pp, 42 repr. supplementary checklist 8 pp

LOS ANGELES COUNTY MUSEUM OF ART, *39 Ink drawings*, 25 April–28 May 1972 (extended to 31 July), with a text by Samuel Beckett, introduction by Barbara Rose and a presentation note by Maurice Tuchman, folder, 1 repr. (cover)

MARLBOROUGH GALLERY, New York, *Ink drawings 1965–1972*, Dec 1972, foreword by Samuel Beckett, introduction by Barbara Rose, 8 pp, folder, 1 repr.

FORT WORTH ART CENTER MUSEUM, *idem*. April–May 1973

CENTRE NATIONAL D'ART CONTEMPORAIN (later MNAM-Centre Pompidou), Paris, 1973, *39 gravures 1970–73*, travelling exhibition catalogue (later increased number of prints), 1974–9, 28 cities in France and 3 in Germany, introduction by André Fermigier, and an interview with Germain Viatte, brochure, 8 pp, 40 repr. (vignette)

THE TEL AVIV MUSEUM, March–April 1973, *Paintings: 1957–1965 and 1968* (retrospective of the abstract period), introduction by Haim Gamzu, brochure, 28 pp, 12 b&w repr., Hebrew and English

MARLBOROUGH FINE ART, London, March 1974, *Drawings, Inks and Etchings*, introduction by Robert Hughes, 30 pp, 64 repr. (mostly vignette)

MARLBOROUGH GALLERY, New York, 11 Oct–1 Nov 1975, *Paintings and Watercolors 1973–1975* (first show of the life-paintings), with a preliminary text by the artist, 24 pp, 13 b&w repr., 6 col.

VICTORIA AND ALBERT MUSEUM, London, Feb–May 1976, *Samuel Beckett by Avigdor Arikha*, foreword by C M Kauffmann, introduction and catalogue by Mordechai Omer brochure, 12 pp, 16 repr.

MARLBOROUGH GALERIE AG, Zürich, April–May 1977, *Ölbilder, Aquarelle und Zeichnungen*, foreword by Samuel Beckett, 20 pp, 9 b&w, 2 col. repr.

ATELIER CROMMELYNCK, *Avigdor Arikha huit gravures*, Paris 1977, 8 collotype reproductions, edition of 500 copies

GALERIE AMSTUTZ, Zürich, autumn 1977, *Huit gravures – Editions de l'Atelier Crommelynck, Paris*, brochure, 12 pp, 8 repr.

MARLBOROUGH FINE ART, London, May–June 1978, *Oil-paintings, Watercolours and Drawings*, interview with Barbara Rose, 20 pp, 9 b&w, 6 col. repr.

NEW 57 GALLERY, Edinburgh, Festival Exhibition, 14 Aug–9 Sept 1978, *Paintings, Drawings and Watercolors*, foreword by Samuel Beckett, 16 pp, 9 b&w, 3 col. repr.

JANIE C LEE GALLERY, Houston, Texas, Feb–March 1979, *Drawings, Watercolors and Paintings*, introduction: interview with Barbara Rose, brochure, 16 pp, 5 col, 2 b&w repr.

THE CORCORAN GALLERY OF ART, Washington DC, 15 June–26 Aug 1979, *Twenty-two Paintings 1974–78*, introduction by Jane Livingston, 40 pp, 18 b&w, 4 col. repr.

MARLBOROUGH GALLERY, New York, 4 Oct–1 Nov 1980, *Recent work*, 44 pp, 5 col, 32 b&w repr.

BERGGRUEN, Paris, 29 May–12 Sept, *Dessins et gravures*, with a text by the artist, 98 pp, 80 repr.

MUSÉE DES BEAUX-ARTS DE DIJON, 29 Mar–28 June 1981, *Arikha*, introduction by Pierre Georgel, 60 pp, 107 b&w repr. (mostly vignette)

MARLBOROUGH FINE ART, London, May–June 1982, *Oil paintings and drawings*, 48 pp, 9 col, 33 b&w repr.

MARLBOROUGH GALLERY, New York, 8 Sept–4 Oct 1983, *Paintings, drawings and pastels*, 14 col, 28 b&w repr.

MARLBOROUGH GALLERY, New York, 8 Nov–4 Dec 1984, *New York drawings*, Jan–May 1984, introduction by Jane Livingston, 36 pp, 36 repr.

MARLBOROUGH GALLERY, New York, 29 May–22 June 1985, *Recent paintings*, 30 pp, 15 col, 10 b&w repr.

TEL AVIV UNIVERSITY GALLERY, Jan–Feb 1986, *Prints 1950–1985*, introduction by Mordechai Omer, reprint of 1974 Robert Hughes introduction, and of 'Avigdor Arikha interviewed by Barbara Rose', second corrected (limited) reprinting, 144 pp, 110 repr.

MARLBOROUGH FINE ART, London, October 1986, *Oil paintings, Pastels and Drawings*, 48 pp, 18 col, 25 b&w repr.

L A LOUVER, Venice, California, 7 April–9 May 1987, with excerpts from texts by Samuel Beckett, Robert Hughes, Barbara Rose, Maurice Tuchman (faulty exhibitions-list and bibliography, two pages errata were printed later), 32 pp, 13 col, 8 b&w repr.

MARLBOROUGH FINE ART LTD, TOKYO, 19 Apr–31 May 1988, *Oils, Watercolours, Pastels, Inks and Drawings*, introduction by Shūji Takashina, 50 pp, 25 col, 7 b&w repr., Japanese and English

MARLBOROUGH GALLERY, New York, October 1988, *Paintings, Pastels and Drawings 1986–1988*, with a text by the artist, 48 pp, 29 col, 10 b&w repr.

MARLBOROUGH FINE ART, London, 14 March–14 April 1990, *Oils, Pastels and Drawings*, 56 pp, 31 col, 16 b&w repr.

MARLBOROUGH GALLERY, New York, 7 May–6 June 1992, *Works 1990–91*, 44 pp, 28 col, 8 b&w repr. + cover

SELECTED ESSAYS, INTRODUCTIONS, ARTICLES AND REVIEWS ABOUT ARIKHA

[Anonymous] 'Mr Avigdor Arikha, a brilliant young painter', *The Times*, London, 27 April 1956

ASHBERY, John: 'Paris Notes', *Art International*, vol V/9, 1961, p 50

BECKETT, Samuel: *Pour Avigdor Arikha*, 1966, Galerie Claude Bernard, Paris, Jan–Feb 1967, exh. announcement. German translation (by Elmar Tophoven) in *Samuel Beckett Auswahl*, Suhrkamp Hausbuch, Frankfurt-am-Main, 1967, p 379. Reprinted in *Avigdor Arikha dessins 1965–1970*, Centre National d'Art Contemporain, Paris, 1970. English version in *Arikha 39 Ink Drawings 1965–1972*, Los Angeles County Museum of Art, April–June 1972; Marlborough Gallery, New York, 1972; Fort Worth Art Center Museum, 1973; French and English versions reprinted in *Samuel Beckett by Avigdor Arikha*, Victoria & Albert Museum, London, 1976; *Avigdor Arikha Ölbilder, Aquarelle, Zeichnungen*, German translation, Marlborough Galerie AG, Zürich, 1977, *Avigdor Arikha – Paintings, Drawings and Watercolors*, New 57 Gallery, Edinburgh, 1978. Samuel Beckett *Disjecta*, Calder, London, 1983, p 152

BECKETT, Samuel: *CEILING* (for A A) in *Arikha*, Paris and London, 1985; French version *PLAFOND*, reprinted: 'En attendant Arikha', in *Le nouvel observateur*, Paris, 18–24 October 1985, pp 102–3

BECKETT, Samuel: an untitled tribute, in *Arikha*, Paris and London, 1985; reprinted in *Lire*, Paris, Feb 1990, p 21

BERRYMAN, Larry: 'Avigdor Arikha – Marlborough Fine Art', *Arts Review*, vol XXXVIII, no 21, London, 24 Oct 1986, p 579

BERRYMAN, Larry: 'Avigdor Arikha', *Arts Review*, vol XLII, no 7, London, 6 April 1990, pp 182–3

BOSQUET, Alain: 'The Illustrations of Avigdor Arikha', *Typographica*, no 13, London, 1957, pp 22–9

BRENSON, Michael: 'A World of Menace from Avigdor Arikha', *The New York Times*, 16 Sept 1983

BRENSON, Michael: 'When Royalty called Arikha', *The New York Times*, 23 Sept 1983

BRENSON, Michael: 'Fresh Vision Based on a Grand Tradition', *The New York Times*, 7 July 1985

BRONOWSKI, Yoram: 'Pegisha im Avigdor Arikha', *Haaretz*, Tel Aviv, 30 Aug 1991 (Hebrew)

BUTCHER, G M: 'What I tried to think was impossible', *Art News and Review*, London, 9 May 1959

CABANNE, Pierre: 'Arikha au bout du miroir', *Combat*, Paris, 14 Dec 1970

CABANNE, Pierre: 'Arikha en noir et blanc', *Le Matin*, Paris, 8 Aug 1980

CASSOU, Jean: introduction to Arikha, *8 lithographies sur le thème de Caïn*, Caractères, Paris, 1955, original edition

CLAIR, Jean: 'Arikha', *L'Express*, Paris, 20–26 Feb 1987, p 107

CLOTHIER, Peter: 'Avigdor Arikha', *Art News*, New York, September 1987, p 155

COMTE, Philippe: review, in *Opus International*, no 23, Paris, Mar 1971, p 54

CORCOS, Pierre: 'Le regard devant les mots', in *Opus*, no 126, Paris, 1991

CORDELLIER, Dominique: in *Raphaël et l'art français*, RMN Grand Palais, Paris, 1983, pp 71–2

CUZIN, Jean-Pierre: 'Tendresse et colère', *Connaissance des arts*, Paris, Oct 1988, no 440, pp 106–14, 9 repr. + cover photograph by Hans Namuth

CUZIN, Jean-Pierre, and Marie-Anne DUPUY in *Copier créer*, exh. cat., Musée du Louvre, Paris, 1993, pp 194–5

DEJEAN, Philippe: 'Avigdor Arikha: le hasard et la nécessité', *Le quotidien de Paris*, 8 Aug 1980

EDELMAN, Robert G: 'Avigdor Arikha at Marlborough', *Art in America*, New York, Dec 1985, pp 129–30

FEALDMAN, Barry: 'A Major Painter of our Time', *The Jewish Chronicle*, London, 18 June 1982

FERMIGIER, André: introduction, travelling exhibition catalogue, *Arikha 39 gravures 1970–1973*, Centre National d'Art Contemporain, Paris, 1973

FERMIGIER, André: 'Arikha à Zurich', *Le Monde*, Paris, 12 May 1977

FERMIGIER, André: 'La bataille de Bédriac', *Le Monde*, Paris, 12 June 1980

FERMIGIER, André: 'La minute de vérité', *Le Monde*, Paris, 5 June 1982

FISCHER, Yona: *Landscape–Abstraction–Nature*, The Israel Museum, Jerusalem, 1972, pp 70, 110–12

FISCHER, Yona: *Masterpieces of The Israel Museum*, Florence, 1985, p 63

FISCHER, Yona: in *Peindre dans la lumière de la Méditerranée*, exh. cat., Israel Museum, Jerusalem, and Musée Cantini, Marseille, 1987, pp 202–3

FOOT, M R D: 'When words stop', *Books and Bookmen*, London, April 1986

FORGEY, Benjamin: 'The Lonely Intensity of Avigdor Arikha Glows at Corcoran Exhibit', *The Washington Star*, Washington, 17 June 1979

FORGEY, Benjamin: 'The Hirshhorn's Big Draw', *The Washington Post*, 15 Mar 1984

FOUCART, Bruno: 'Arikha au Musée des Beaux-Arts de Dijon – La leçon de peinture', *Le Monde*, Paris, 12 June 1981

FRÉMON, Jean: 'Arikha, une frémissante lucidité', *Politique-Hebdo*, Paris, 31 Dec 1970

GAGE, Edward: 'Innately Honest Vision of Arikha', *The Scotsman*, Edinburgh, 31 Aug 1978

GALY-CARLES, Henri: 'Arikha', *Aujourd'hui*, no 34, Paris, Dec 1961, p 42

GAMZU, Haim: introduction, *Avigdor Arikha, Paintings: 1957–1965 and 1968*, The Tel Aviv Museum, 1973

GEORGEL, Pierre: introduction to *Arikha*, Musée des Beaux-Arts, Dijon, 1981

GERRIT, H: 'Avigdor Arikha at Marlborough', *Art in America*, New York, March 1981, pp 129–30

GETTINGS, Frank: *Drawings 1974–1984*, Hirshhorn Museum, Washington, 1984, pp 18, 30–37

GLABERSON, Barbara: 'Arikha's Classicism', *Art World*, New York, Oct 1983

GOSLING, Nigel: 'Artist in the Wrong Role?', *The Observer*, London, 24 Feb 1974

HICKS, Alistair: 'Dark Areas', *The Spectator*, London, 4 Oct 1986

HOFSTADTER, Dan: 'A Painting Dervish' (Profiles), *The New Yorker*, New York, 1 June 1987, pp 37–56; idem: slightly revised in *Temperaments – Artists Facing their Work*, Knopf, New York, 1992, pp 94–122

HOFSTADTER, Dan: 'Ingres in New York', *The New Criterion*, vol 5, no 5, Jan 1987, pp 17–21

HOLMES, Anne: 'Artist Gives up Abstraction for Existential Realism', *Houston Chronicle*, 26 Dec 1974

HUGHES, Robert: 'Feedback from Life', *Time*, 7 May 1973, p 38

HUGHES, Robert: introduction to *Avigdor Arikha: Inks, Drawings and Etchings*, Marlborough Fine Art, London, 1974

HUGHES, Robert: 'Arikha's Elliptical Intensity', *Time*, 30 July 1979, p 71

HUGHES, Robert: in *The Shock of the New*, New York, 1980, pp 404–5

JAFFE, M C L: 'Arikha', *Quadrum*, vol 9, Brussels, 1960, pp 144–5

JOHNSON, PATRICIA: 'Works by two artists with sharply contrasting visions', *Houston Chronicle*, 18 May 1986

JOUFFROY, Alain: 'Arikha', *Arts*, Paris, 12 Oct 1955

KINMOTH, Patrick: 'Arikha: A Poetic Artist', *Vogue*, London, Oct 1986

KITAJ, R B: 'Arikha', *RA – The Magazine for the Friends of the Royal Academy*, no 12, London, autumn 1986, p 41

KRAMER, Hilton: Untitled review, *The New York Times*, 21 Dec 1972

LAP SZE TO: 'The Painter for Painters II – interview with Avigdor Arikha', in *Twenty-first Century Bimonthly* (Chinese), The Chinese University of Hong Kong, vol 6, Aug 1991, pp 58–68 (with repr., some inverted, col. repr. of *Sam's Spoon*, 1990, on back cover (Chinese)

LEISER, Erwin: 'Die Eroberung der Wirklichkeit', *Du*, Zürich, June 1987, pp 80–85

LIVINGSTON, Jane: *Thoughts on Avigdor Arikha*, introduction, The Corcoran Gallery of Art, Washington, 1979

LIVINGSTON, Jane: introduction, *Arikha, New York Drawings*, Marlborough Gallery, New York, 1984

LIVINGSTONE, Marco: 'Arikha', *The Burlington Magazine*, London, Oct 1986, no 1003, vol CXXVIII, pp 757–8

LUCIE-SMITH, Edward: 'Avigdor Arikha', *Art and Artists*, London, May 1982, pp 36–7

MCCORQUODALE, Charles: 'Samuel Beckett by Avigdor Arikha', *Art International*, vol XX 4–5, April–May 1976, pp 41–2

MCCORQUODALE, Charles: 'Avigdor Arikha – a Tribute to Samuel Beckett', *The Connoisseur*, London, May 1976

MAURIES, Patrick: 'Avigdor Arikha, textes et interviews', *Libération*, Paris, 13 Dec 1985

MELOT, Michel; BOURET, Claude; BOURET, Blandine: *La lithographie en France des origines à nos jours*, Fondation Nationale des Arts Graphiques et Plastiques, Paris, 1982, pp 207, 234

MICHEL, Jacques: 'Arikha, le retour au dessin réaliste', *Le Monde*, Paris, 6 Jan 1971

MICHEL, Jacques: 'Des peintres qui peignent', *Le Monde*, Paris, 4 Nov 1976

MITCHELL, Breon: *Beyond Illustration: The Livre d'Artiste in the Twentieth Century*, The Lilly Library, Indiana University, Bloomington, 1976, pp 53, 72, 83

MUCHNIC, Suzanne: 'His Passion: Painting from Life', *Los Angeles Times*, Calendar, 9 April, 1987, part VI, pp 1 and 4

NAGEL, C U: 'Radierungen von Arikha in Institut Français', *Aachener Volkszeitung*, Aachen, 14 Feb 1979

NARKISS, Mordecai: announcement preface *Avigdor Arikha – peintures, dessins, bois*, Le Musée National Bézalel, Jerusalem, 1953

NEWS: The National Galleries of Scotland News, Edinburgh, Sept–Oct 1983

OMER, Mordechai: introduction *Samuel Beckett by Avigdor Arikha*, Victoria & Albert Museum, London, 1976

OMER, Mordechai: 'Avigdor Arikha: Face to Face towards Life and Still Life', introduction to *Avigdor Arikha, Prints 1950–1985*, The University Gallery, Tel Aviv University, 1986 (Hebrew and English)

OTT, Günther: 'Beckett mit Weinglass, Ausstellung im französichen Institut', *Kölnische Rundschau*, Cologne, 7 Jan 1979

PEPPIATT, Michael: 'Fièvre œil-main', *Connaissance des arts*, Paris, May 1982, pp 62–9

PEPPIATT, Michael: 'Avigdor Arikha: A Hunger in the Eye', *Art International*, vol XXV/7–8, Sept–Oct 1982, pp 18–28

PERRY-LEHMANN, Meira: *One Hundred Works on Paper from the Collection of The Israel Museum*, Geneva, 1986, pp 140–41

PICARD, Denis: 'Regards avec Arikha', *Connaissance des arts*, Paris, Oct 1985

QUANTRILL, Malcolm: 'London Letter', *Art International*, vol XXI/5–6, 1978, pp 50–51

ROETHLISBERGER, Marcel: 'Arikha écrits sur l'art', *Connaissance des arts*, Paris, May 1992, pp 62–7

ROHDE, Peter P: brochure preface, *Avigdor Arikha: Tegninger, Grafic og Bogkunst*, Athenaeum Kunsthandel, Copenhagen, 1955

RONNEN, Meir: 'Voices of Silence', *Art News*, New York, Nov 1979, pp 152–3

ROSE, Barbara: catalogue introduction *Avigdor Arikha Dessins 1965–1970*, Centre National d'Art Contemporain, Paris, Dec 1970–Jan 1971. Revised version: 'Inks by Arikha', Introduction, *Arikha: 39 Ink drawings 1965–1972*, Los Angeles County Museum of Art 1972; Marlborough Gallery, New York, 1972; Fort Worth Art Center Museum, 1973

ROSE, Barbara: review, in *New York Magazine*, 1 Jan 1973

ROSE, Barbara: 'Talking about Art: Washington DC as Capital of Art', *Vogue*, New York, Aug 1979

ROUVE, Pierre: 'Startling Confluence', *Art News and Review*, vol VIII, no 6, London, 14 April 1956

RUGOFF, Ralph: 'Art-pick of the week', *LA Weekly*, Los Angeles, 13–17 Apr, 1987

RUSSELL, John: 'Avigdor Arikha', review, *The New York Times*, 14 Oct 1988

SCHIFF, Fritz: 'Avigdor Arikha veomanuto shel dor hadash', *Mevooth*, Tel Aviv, Nov 1953 (Hebrew)

SELDIS, Henry J: 'Works by Arikha Painter and Scholar on Display', *The Los Angeles Times* (Calendar), 21 May 1972

SELDIS, Henry J: 'European Art Filling in the Gap', *The Los Angeles Times* (Calendar), 12 Oct 1975

SHANNON, Joseph: 'Proximate Vision', *Art in America*, New York, May 1982, pp 101–5

STEVENS, Mark: 'The Art of Ambush', *Newsweek*, 2 July 1979, pp 84–5

STEVENS, Mark: 'The Rights of the Eye', *The New Republic*, Washington, 13 and 20 July, pp 40–42

STONE, Peter: 'From Life', *Jewish Chronicle*, London, 24 Feb 1974

TAKASHINA, Shûji: *Resonance of the Spirit in Arikha*, catalogue introduction, Marlborough Fine Art, Tokyo, 1988 (Japanese and English)

TAMMUZ, Binyamin: 'Tsiurei Arikha leRilke', *Haaretz*, Tel Aviv, 20 Mar 1953 (Hebrew)

THOMSON, Duncan: in *Great Scots*, Scottish National Portrait Gallery, HMSO, Edinburgh, 1984, pp 1, 70

THOMSON, Duncan: 'Duncan Thomson Talks to Avigdor Arikha', *Modern Painters*, London, May 1990, vol 3, no 1, pp 108–9

TUCK, Lon: 'Drawing the Line at Abstract Art – The Commonplace Subjects and Bold Brushstrokes of Avigdor Arikha', *The Washington Post*, 16 June 1979, section B, pp 1–2

VIATTE, Germain: entry on 'Studio Interior with Mirror, 1987' in *L'art moderne à Marseille, la collection du Musée Cantini*, 1988, p 200

WOIMANT, Françoise: 'Arikha', *Les nouvelles de l'estampe*, Bibliothèque Nationale, Paris, 1975, pp 20–22

ZALMONA, Ygal: 'Avigdor Arikha's "Going Out"', *The Israel Museum Journal*, Jerusalem, 1984, vol III, pp 85–6

MARLBOROUGH

LONDON

Marlborough Fine Art (London) Ltd.
6 Albemarle Street
London WIX 4BY
Telephone: 071-629 5161
Telefax: 071-629 6338

NEW YORK

Marlborough Gallery, Inc.
40 West 57th Street
New York, NY 10019
Telephone: 1-212-541 4900
Telefax: 1-212-541 4948

TOKYO

Marlborough Fine Art Ltd. Tokyo
Ginza AH Building 4th Floor
3-5, Ginza 4-chome
Chuo-ku
Tokyo 104
Telephone: 81-3-3563 5884
Telefax: 81-3-3563 5872

MADRID

Galería Marlborough, S.A.
Orfila 5
28010 Madrid
Telephone: 34-1-319 1414
Telefax: 34-1-308 4345

Catalogue no. 470
ISBN 0 900955 45 7

Designed by Derek Birdsall and
produced by Omnific Studios/London
Printed in England by
Balding + Mansell

© 1994 Marlborough

LONDON

Agents for

Frank Auerbach
Christopher Bramham
Steven Campbell
Lynn Chadwick
Stephen Conroy
Christopher Couch
John Davies
Dieter Hacker
Bill Jacklin
Ken Kiff
R.B. Kitaj
Christopher Le Brun
Raymond Mason
Henry Moore
Sidney Nolan
Thérèse Oulton
Victor Pasmore
Celia Paul
John Piper
Paula Rego
The Estate of Francis Bacon
The Estate of Barbara Hepworth
The Estate of Oskar Kokoschka
The Estate of Kurt Schwitters
The Estate of Graham Sutherland

IMPORTANT WORKS AVAILABLE BY
Impressionists and Post-Impressionists
Twentieth Century European Masters
German Expressionists
Post War American Artists

Modern Masters and
Contemporary Graphics
available from
Marlborough Graphics Ltd.

NEW YORK

Agents for

Magdalena Abakanowicz
John Alexander
Avigdor Arikha
Fernando Botero
Claudio Bravo
Grisha Bruskin
Vincent Desiderio
Richard Estes
Red Grooms
Alex Katz
Marisol
Larry Rivers
Altoon Sultan
James Surls
Neil Welliver
The Estate of Jacques Lipchitz
The Estate of James Rosati

MADRID

Agents for

Juan Genovés
Luis Gordillo
Francisco Leiro
Antonio López García
Lucio Muñoz
Daniel Quintero
Manolo Valdés